A quick word on colouring

Let your imagination run wild.

Don't necessarily pick real life colours, pick whatever colours YOU like best! Colouring and drawing is the perfect way to explore one's creative expression. You make all decisions, and our Ultimate Colouring Books aim to encourage unlimited creativity and fantasy. There are no wrong choices!

Coloured Pencils are your best option.

While developing our books we identified coloured pencils as the best choice for a happy colouring experience with great results:
they teach you how much pressure to use when holding a pen and support the improvement of handwriting.
they are very versatile and you can get the in an unlimited amount of different colours.
they come in different thicknesses. We found that the use of thick and/or triangular shaped pencils gives children the best grip. It makes colouring easier, leads to nicer results and thus gives the kids more confidence.
practicing the use of pencil sharpeners will help your child's fine motor skills.
unwanted results can be changed easily and the use of an eraser can be improved.

Crayons

Pure beeswax crayons for toddlers or gel crayons for older kids are good for little hands since they don't need to apply pressure. Crayons do however tend to smudge, and also seem to regularly find their way onto furniture, clothes and into the washing machine where they melt into the laundry.

Felt Pens & Markers

Our colouring books are printed on quality 90 gsm paper with a nice smooth surface. We've tried a variety of felt pens and markers and found those with heavy ink flow might bleed through or run into one another, since kids tend to have a slightly heavier hand when colouring with them. They also make it more difficult to experiment with blending and layering different colours.

Watercolours

We've also tried the use of watercolours and watercolour pencils and the results were fine in our colouring books. Just make sure to use a hard surface under the current page.

Tip: If you like it cheap and simple, we recommend to use coated cardboard such as a broken-down single side of a cereal box under the colouring page!

Finally, be proud of what you created and feel free to share your masterpieces on Amazon for us all to see! We love seeing the results of your creativity and how much pleasure kids and adults alike are getting out of working with our illustrations. if you have any questions, suggestions or ideas for our upcoming publications, we are happy to receive your email at jdePublishing@gmail.com.

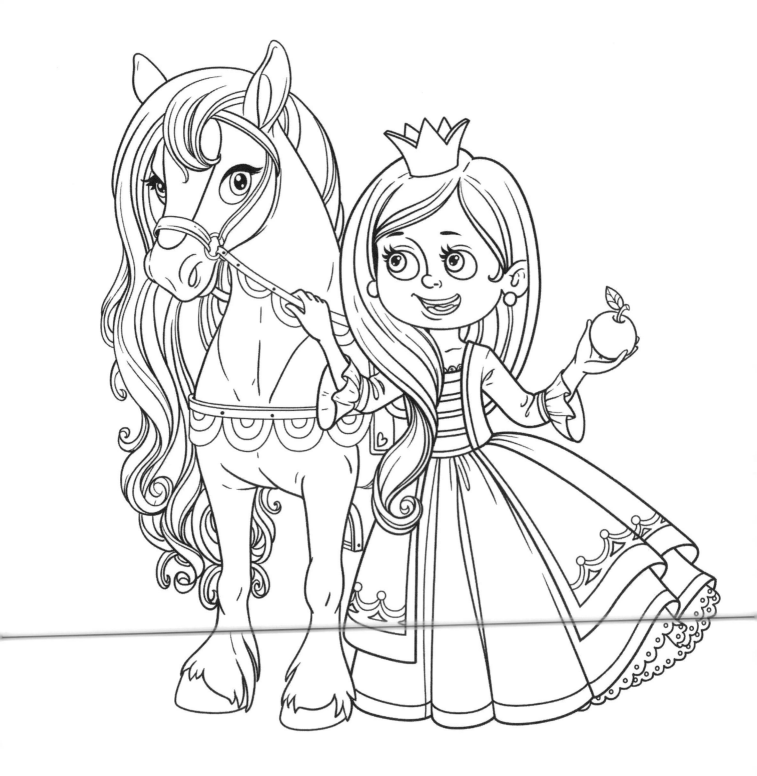

First published as paperback by JDE Publishing in 2020

ISBN: 978-3-949053-97-9

We're happy to receive your feedback and suggestions:
jdePublishing@gmail.com

55558743R00063